Scottish Borders from Above

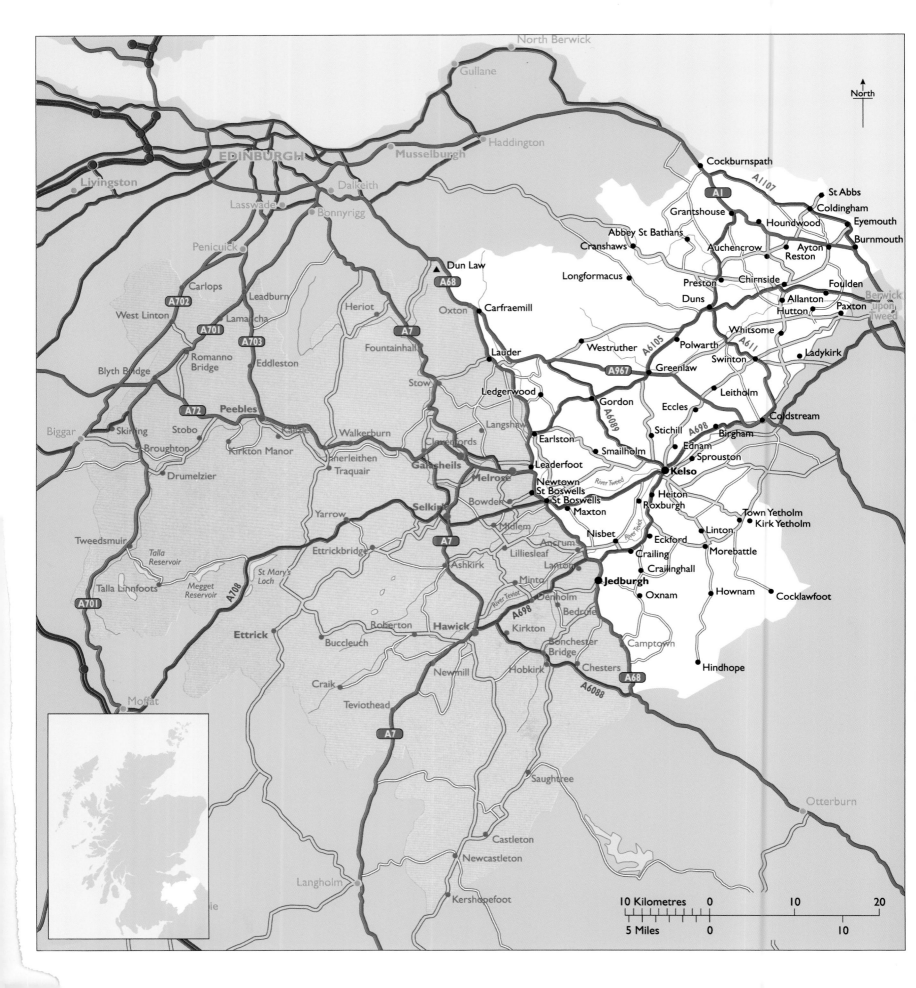

ALASTAIR CAMPBELL

Scottish Borders from Above

ALBUM ONE – EAST

DEVERON
PUBLICATIONS

This book is dedicated to Margaret, Fiona, Karen and Lorna, my wife and daughters

First published in 2006 by

DEVERON
PUBLICATIONS

Academy House,
Shedden Park Road,
Kelso TD5 7AL

Reprinted 2007

ISBN 10: 0-9553110-0-4
ISBN 13: 978-0-9553110-0-0

British Library Cataloguing-in-Publication Data

A catalogue record of this book is available on request

Book and jacket designed by Mark Blackadder

Printed and bound in Singapore by Tien Wah Press Pte. Ltd.

Introduction and Acknowledgements

The *Scottish Borders*, one of 32 local government unitary council areas of Scotland, encompasses the eastern half of the Southern Uplands and the valley of the 156km River Tweed. The Berwickshire coast is the eastern boundary; East and Midlothian are to the north; South Lanarkshire and Dumfries and Galloway to the west and finally England's border regions of Cumbria and Northumberland are along its southern edge. It has a population of approximately 109,000 (2005) and an area of 4732 sq km.

The area covers the former counties of Berwickshire, Peeblesshire, Roxburghshire and Selkirkshire, as well as part of Midlothian. More recently, in 1975, the area was created as a two-tier region with the districts of Berwickshire, Ettrick and Lauderdale, Roxburgh and Tweeddale. In 1996 the region became a unitary authority area and the districts were wound up. The name *Scottish Borders* dates from 1996 with the creation of the modern council area.

My reason for producing this first album of mostly aerial photographs, is that the area presents a diverse landscape and when viewed from above, a rare insight is provided. The aerial views of towns, villages, valleys and historical sites, record their development.

The task of researching photographs for *Scottish Borders from Above* to reflect the history and geography of the area, soon made me aware of the volume of photographic material that is archived both locally and nationally. It proved impossible to include the whole area in one book, hence the series of two books, *Album One* and *Album Two*. The main north to south artery, the A68 road, provides the dividing line for the two publications.

The arrangement of the material in *Album One* has been organised alphabetically for ease of reference. The east area includes seven towns, Coldstream, Duns, Earlston, Eyemouth, Jedburgh, Kelso and Lauder all of which have a good selection of photographs. Hence the layout reflects the number of images available for the different centres of population.

The colour photographs mostly record the last ten to fifteen years, with some exceptions from the national archives. A number of 'ground photographs' are included to add to the history of the communities and when aerial images were not available for publication.

My search led me to these main sources; Scottish Borders Council (SBC); the collections of the National Monuments Record of Scotland (NMRS), the archive of the Royal Commission on the Ancient and Historical Monuments of Scotland (RCAHMS); the Scottish Cultural Resource Archive Network (scran).

Scottish Borders Council has been the source of the most recent colour photographs and I acknowledge the assistance I received from the staff at Newtown St Boswells.

A number of the towns have Royal Air Force vertical and oblique aerial photographs of the 1940s and 1950s, that are held in NMRS. Those images contributed to the Scottish part of the National Survey of Great Britain undertaken by the Royal Air Force, to support the Ordnance Survey with their map revision during the post-war years. I am indebted to the staff in the RCAHMS library for their guidance while I accessed the numerous file boxes of their extensive collection. My personal thanks go to Rebecca Bailey, Lesley Ferguson and Kristina Watson who, along with Dave Easton provided advice and practical support with the material, from this national archive.

The Scottish Cultural Resource Archive Network (scran) has generated a collection of resources both photographic and audio that reflect all aspects of our national heritage. I thank Neil Fraser for his assistance in tracing both aerial and ground images. You will note that a number of the photographs have references to the scran audio collection. This audio link, provides a unique dimension to this publication, as it permits access to broadcast radio programmes, presented by myself from the studio of BBC Radio Tweed in Selkirk, from 1983 to the early 1990s. I am indebted to BBC Radio Scotland, Scottish Borders Council and Scottish Borders Digby Project, led by Wendy Ball who together made possible the digitising of over fifty programmes. These programmes may be accessed, *free of charge*, via the scran web site at most local authority libraries, including Scottish Borders. When accessed from home, a small registration fee will be requested.

In addition to the assistance I have gained from the main resource archives I am grateful to a number of other people who have provided information and material, they include; Robert D Clapperton Photographic Trust, National Library of Scotland, Reston Primary School, Roxburghe Estates, Scottish Borders Archive & Local History Centre, University of St Andrews Library, VisitScotland Borders, Alex Blair, Ian Campbell, Cathy Chick, Helen Darling, John Dent, Reg Fairbairn, Jim Lewis, Dave Little, Robert Millican, Andrew Mercer, Rory MacDonald, Jimmy Oliver, Keith Robeson, Scott Wardlaw, Sheila Whitehead and former colleagues at BBC Radio Tweed.

Presenting the Scottish Borders through photographs also provides the opportunity to acknowledge the many talented photographers of the past one hundred years. As pioneers of their craft, they, thankfully, had the foresight to photograph the development of the area in the early 20th century, capturing everyday images to provide their unique record. In more recent times, with the use of aircraft and high quality equipment, aerial images have captured a new perspective to this Border land.

On completion of my research, book designer Mark Blackadder imaginatively produced the page and cover design, thus transforming an idea into a book, while Eve Webster dealt efficiently with all other aspects of the production. I'm most grateful for their advice, without which this publication would not have become a reality.

Finally, I thank Margaret my wife, for her support and encouragement, along with the other members of my extended family who have assisted with this project.

ALASTAIR CAMPBELL   2006

Audio clips linked to communities

The text describing some of the communities will have this symbol 🎧. It acts as a reminder that an audio recording associated with the community or the individual can be accessed via www.scran.ac.uk. The audio clips are recordings of programmes produced at BBC Radio Tweed's studio in Selkirk, between 1983 and the early 1990s.

Listed below are the programmes, along with a reference number, that relate to this publication and *Album Two*. Programmes may be accessed by keying in the name printed in bold.

1. **Abernethy, Ian:** Heiton, local historian (1990)
2. **Aitchison, Henry:** Lochton Farm, Birgham (1984)
3. **Ancrum:** Kath Anderson, Ian Kennedy, Mike Povey, John Rogerson, Lizzie Smart, Jeannie Stewart and Rob Taylor (1992)
4. **Barr, John:** Farmer – 102 years (1990)
5. **Blair, Sandy:** retired Kelso Jeweller (1984)
6. **Blake, Dorothy:** Lady's Maid (1990)
7. **Bowden:** Janette Chalmers, Tony Chaplin, Mary Cunningham, Jessie MacDonald, Janet Symington and Rev. James Watson (1994)
8. **Broughton:** Neil Brownlee, Graham Buchanan – Dunlop, Alistair Bruce, Rev. John Rennie and David Younger. (1990)
9. **Chirnside:** programme number 1: Mary Dippy, Mame Prentice and Cynthia Swan (1989)
10. **Chirnside:** programme number 2: George Campbell, Rev. Peter Graham and Bobby Turner (1989)
11. **Clovenfords:** Gardeners Stan Anderson and Jimmy Moffat (1989)
12. **Coldstream:** Jim Davidson, Alastair Marjoribanks, Rev. Ian Penman, Jean Scott, Bert Tocher and Henry Walker (1991)
13. **Cowan, Andrew:** World Champion Rally Driver (1984)
14. **Craig, Alex:** Eyemouth fisherman / skipper (1989)
15. **Crombie, Chrissie:** Lady's Maid (1989)
16. **Cruickshank, Jim:** Clovenfords – Clydesdale horse enthusiast(1989)
17. **Davies, Doug:** Ashkirk farmer, curling internationalist and international rugby player and Sandy Thorburn (1987)
18. **Eddleston:** Willie Bertram, Jane Holmes, Willie Wilson, Rev. David McFarlane, Lawrie McTeer, Pat Nicholson and Margaret Smart (1992)
19. **Euman, Bob:** Innerleithen piper (1989)
20. **Fleming, Jean:** Morebattle local historian (1990)

ROYAL COMMISSION ON THE ANCIENT AND
HISTORICAL MONUMENTS OF SCOTLAND

The publisher acknowledges the assistance of the
Royal Commission on the Ancient and Historical
Monuments of Scotland (RCAHMS) in the
production of this volume.

Many of the images in this volume have been
selected from the RCAHMS collections. RCAHMS is
responsible for collecting, recording and interpreting
information on the architectural, industrial, archaeological and maritime heritage of Scotland. Whether
you are working, teaching, studying or simply
exploring your local heritage, RCAHMS resources
are available to assist your research. Included in those
resources is the national collection of aerial
photography of Scotland that comprises over one
million images, ranging in date from 1944 to 2000.
The images have come from sources including the
Royal Air Force, Ordnance Survey, private companies
and the Luftwaffe, as well as from RCAHMS's own
flying programme. An appointment is required to
consult this collection.

RCAHMS
John Sinclair House
16 Bernard Terrace
Edinburgh, EH8 9NX

Telephone: +44 (0)131 662 1456
Email: info@rcahms.gov.uk
Website: www.rcahms.gov.uk

Public search room open
Monday – Friday, 9.30am – 4.30pm

SCOTTISH CULTURAL RESOURCE
ARCHIVE NETWORK (SCRAN)

Scran is an educational charity providing educational
access to digital materials representing Scotland's culture
and history. The site contains 330,000 images, movies and
sound clips from museums, galleries, archives and the
media.

All local authority schools in Scotland have full access
to scran through support from the Scottish Executive as
do many public libraries. All universities and most colleges
in Scotland are subscribers, along with a host of cultural
institutions, community and home users throughout the
UK and beyond.

The organisation was originally set up as a
membership body with over 100 project partners including
National Museums of Scotland, National Library of
Scotland, Royal Commission on the Ancient and Historic
Monuments of Scotland, Scottish Museums Council,
Historic Scotland, Glasgow Museums and Art Galleries
and many local collections in museums, galleries, archives
and universities.Funding came from the Millennium
Commission and New Opportunity Fund to enable grant-
aid to organisations to permit the digitisation of national
treasures.

All the resources on scran are freely viewable up to the
thumbnail level, licensed subscribers have access to the full
screen sized images and the right to use the material for
educational purposes. An annual Home Users Subscription
is available and can be purchased by visiting the site or by
contacting Neil Fraser, neil.fraser@scran.ac.uk or telephone
+ 44 (0) 131 662 1211

Website: www.scran.ac.uk

Scottish Borders from Above

ABBEY ST BATHANS 1998

(*Below left*) 8km north-west of Duns this isolated spot sees the Whiteadder Water flowing close to the village. It was here that St Bathan, the cousin of St Columba, is thought to have founded a cell in the sixth century. There was also a convent of Cistercian nuns and part of the 12th century Priory Church is incorporated in the Parish Church. The circular tanks of the trout farm and Abbey St Bathan's House to the left, can be seen within the long evening shadows. © *Scottish Borders Council*

AUCHENCROW 2006

(*Left*) A small village 3km west of Reston in Berwickshire. Possibly this unusual place name came from the Gaelic, Auch na Craw, meaning 'valley fields', later corrupted to Auchen.

ALLANTON 1997

(*Below*) 2km from Chirnside, this village lies to the south of the confluence of the Whiteadder and Blackadder Waters. The Blackadder enters from top right to flow beneath the 1851 bridge to join the Whiteadder, out of picture. The road heads south, up through the village towards Whitsome. © *Scottish Borders Council*

AYTON CASTLE 1996

10km north-west of Berwick-upon-Tweed, south of Ayton Village. The founding of a castle by the Anglo-Norman De Vescies in the 12th century, was the beginning of settlement in this area. The castle was destroyed in 1498 and then followed by a second castle that was razed to the ground in 1834. A castellated mansion in red sandstone, Ayton Castle, was built in 1851 for William Mitchell Innes, Governor of the Bank of Scotland. Extensive interior decoration was undertaken in the mid 1870s. Top right can be seen the A1 road that has bypassed nearby Ayton Village since the early 1980s.
© *Scottish Borders Council*

AYTON VILLAGE 1996

10km north-west of Berwick-upon-Tweed, a settlement since the early 12th century, built high above the deep valley of the Eye Water. The former route of the Great North Road (A1) winds its way north with the road to Eyemouth heading east at the base of the photograph .© *Scottish Borders Council*

BEMERSYDE HOUSE
c.1963

In the shadow of Scott's View overlooking the Tweed. The Haig family's hereditary home for over 800 years had Field-Marshall Douglas Haig as its most distinguished occupant until his death in 1928. The original house was built to protect the Monk's Ford, equidistant from Melrose Abbey and Dryburgh Abbey. Rebuilt in 1581, the house has undergone numerous alterations over the last four hundred years, with the most recent being in the 1960s.
© The Scotsman Publications Ltd / Licensed via www.scran.ac.uk

WILLIAM WALLACE

South of Bemersyde overlooking the River Tweed stands the first public statue to William Wallace, erected by the Earl of Buchan, in 1814. Sculpted by John Smith, the Darnick mason and builder who also built the house of Abbotsford for Sir Walter Scott. The figure is 6.5 m and with the plinth, totals 9.1 m. As one of Scotland's greatest national heroes, it was Wallace who led the Scottish resistance, against the tyranny of Edward I, during the Wars of Independence. He was executed in London in 1305. *© Padeapix / Licensed via www.scran.ac.uk*

BIRGHAM 1994

Situated on the north side of the River Tweed, 6km west of Coldstream, where a bridge was evident until the Middle Ages. It was in this village in March 1290 that negotiations to arrange a marriage between the six-year old Queen Margaret of Norway, and the five-year old future Edward II of England took place. The deal was that Edward I guaranteed the survival of Scotland, though to be ruled in partnership. The resulting plan, the Treaty of Birgham, suggested by Alexander III six years earlier, was invalidated by the Maid's early death.

Birgham today is a community with an expanding house base. The Coldstream, Kelso road can be seen right to left. © *Scottish Borders Council*

BURNMOUTH HARBOUR C,1950

(*Below*) Fishermen here were mainly occupied in catching herring and haddock. Maintaining and drying nets was a basic task for centuries, originally in designated fields close to shore. Then drying poles were used from the early nineteenth century, as can be seen in this photograph. © *National Museums of Scotland / Licensed via www.scran.ac.uk*

BURNMOUTH 1997

A small fishing community at the base of 100m cliffs, 10km north west of Berwick-upon-Tweed. In 1600, all that existed was a mill at the burn mouth, hence the name. The harbour was built in 1830 followed by the building of a station at the top of the cliffs by the North British Railway in 1846. The station closed in 1962. The main Scotland-England east coast railway line sweeps round and out of the picture, bottom left, heading towards the Border. The main A1 trunk road can be seen above the railway.
© *Scottish Borders Council*

ENGLAND AND BEYOND 1994

The A68 road skirts Wauchope Forest as it twists up towards the Border and Carter Bar, before heading downhill, south into England and through upper Redesdale towards Catcleugh Reservoir in the distance.
© *Scottish Borders Council*

CARTER BAR C.1952

15km south of Jedburgh on the A68 this is Scotland's gateway in the Cheviot Hills where spectacular views encompass both sides of the National Border. It was here in 1575 that the Redeswire Fray, one of the last battles fought between the English and Scots, took place. A violent battle broke out between a Warden of the English Marches and the Keeper of Liddesdale. At the end of the fray the English, who were largely unarmed, came off worst. Back in the early 1950s there was time to admire the view, enjoy a cup of tea and give one Ford Prefect, in the foreground, a rest before it headed south.
Courtesy of Scottish Borders Archive & Local History Centre

CARTER BAR. BOUNDARY, ENGLAND-SCOTLAND (1371 FT.)

CHARTERHALL AIRFIELD 1999

In the 1940s this was one of two airfields used by the RAF in Berwickshire, the other being Winfield, north of the Tweed near Norham. Both formed the headquarters for 54 OUT (Operational Training Unit) It was at this disused airfield that Jim Clark the farmer's son from Edington Mains near Chirnside, drove Ian Scott Watson's Porche to his first victory in the Border Motor Racing Club Trophy in October 1957. From this early success Clark progressed to be World Motor Racing Champion in 1963 and 1965. After a total of 25 Grand Prix victories including a victory in the Indianapolis 500 in 1965, the Berwickshire farmer's son was tragically killed in April 1968 at Hockenheim, Germany. Charterhall now hosts a stage of the established annual Jim Clark Memorial Rally, in July.
Crown copyright: RCAHMS

CHARTERHALL AIRFIELD 1942. HANGERS AND TECHNICAL AREA

RAF WWII Collection / RCAHMS

  CHIRNSIDE 1999

This T-plan village is 150m above sea level and 15km west of Berwick-upon-Tweed. Its situation is north of the Whiteadder Water, overlooking the valley of the River Tweed and the distant Cheviot Hills south of the Border. The name is thought to be derived from the Cairn which stood on the hill at the east end of the village, known previously as Harelaw Hill. The Duns to Ayton road travels through the Main Street along the top of the village, left to right in the photograph. The Crosshill runs from the right, towards the bottom left corner via the edge of the ploughed field. It then passes the Church and graveyard at the left-hand corner, to meet the main road to Berwick-upon-Tweed. © *Scottish Borders Council*

 JIM CLARK

(*Left*) Jim Clark stops off in Chirnside in 1965 while on a celebratory tour around the Borders. Jim's father is in the foreground, on the extreme right. Sitting next to him is Nancy McBain the sister of Jock McBain, the founder of Border Reivers. © *The Scotsman Publications Ltd / Licensed via www.scran.ac.uk*

CHIRNSIDE PRIMARY SCHOOL 1998

The large white building of Chirnside Primary School, built in 1937, sits in the south east corner of the village. Within the adjacent churchyard is the Parish Church with a Norman doorway, the only remaining feature from the original 12th century Kirk on the same site. The burial ground is the resting place of Jim Clark (1936–68) World Motor Racing Champion 1963 and 1965. © *Scottish Borders Council*

CLINTMAINS

(*Below*) Close to Mertoun House this small village is 3km east of St Boswells and was originally built for the workers of Mertoun Estate. Its name stems from 'the farm by the lake'. © *Scottish Borders Council*

COCKBURNSPATH 1996

At the north east corner of Berwickshire, this ancient village is known locally as Copath. It stands between the ravine of the Dunglass Burn and the twin gorges of the Heriot Water and Pease Burn, all within a short walk to the coastal cliffs of Berwickshire. The characteristic east coast red pantiled roofs are a feature. Towards the top of the photograph, at the end of the main street is the square. Since 1984 this conservation village has been a most welcome site to walkers who are about to complete the 341km Southern Upland Way, Scotland's coast to coast footpath, from Portpatrick to this Border terminus. © *Scottish Borders Council*

COCKBURNSPATH, THE SQUARE 1954

In the square can be seen the medieval Mercat Cross, the first to show the Thistle and Rose as a public emblem. Erected in 1503 by King James VI of Scotland in celebration of his marriage to Princes Mary Tudor, to whom he presented the lands of Cockburnspath as a dowry. The Princess was the sister of King Henry VIII of England and his union of the Tudor Rose and the Scots Thistle was to mark the start of a new and lasting peace. However, Flodden in 1513 upset this plan! *Courtesy of Scottish Borders Archive & Local History Centre*

COLDINGHAM 1997

Coldingham, close to St Abbs on the Berwickshire coast. Coldingham Priory, centre left, was built around 1147 and was burned by the English in 1544 with most of the remainder being demolished by Cromwell in 1648. The village was recorded as a settlement in the 18th century, on the main coast road that exits bottom right. The road, top right, heads towards St Abbs. The caravan park, right, confirms the area's popularity for holidays. A track from the caravan park, links to Coldingham Sands, a popular leisure beach.
© *Scottish Borders Council*

BRIDGE STREET C.1930

Devoid of pavements, still a feature today. *Reproduced courtesy of RCAHMS / R S Henderson collection*

Bridge Street, Coldingham.   224/18

COLDINGHAM SANDS 1998

South of St Abbs, this beach is
overlooked by houses and a hotel.
The local Scottish Youth Hostel
Association building commands
a sea view on the right.
© *Scottish Borders Council*

It was the junction of the River Leet and River Tweed that provided the first major ford upstream from Berwick-upon-Tweed. As a strategic crossing point, the area developed in importance through the centuries as major Scottish and English armies invaded each other's territories by way of the ford. Reminders that there was once a 12th century Cistercian Priory, close to the Market Square, can be seen today through names such as Nun's Walk, Abbey Road and Penitent's Walk. Smeaton's Bridge, completed in 1767 generated the communities development and continues to have a major impact on the area. The town is known world wide because it gave its name to the second oldest Regiment of Foot Guards, The Coldstream Guards. *Reproduced by permission of the Trustees of the National Library of Scotland*

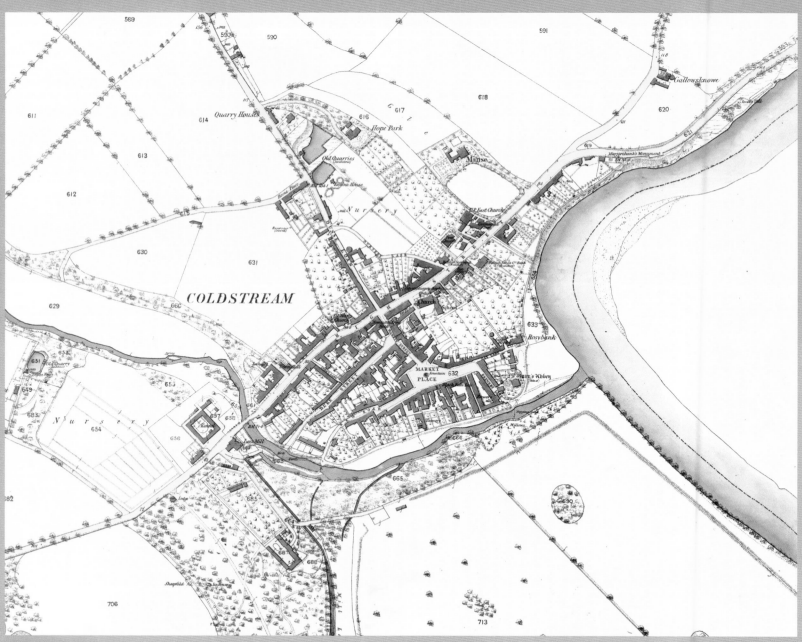

COLDSTREAM 1950

This view looks north with the Duns road heading towards Swintonmill. The High Street can be seen from right to left across the photograph. The set of buildings to the right of the Market Square at the base of the photograph, with the central area seen as a triangle, is the Coldstream Brewery. Across the road to the right sits the Gas Works with the cylindrical Gasometer. The large white building on the right of the Duns Road, was owned by J. Rutherford & Sons, agricultural engineers. Further up the Duns Road, again on the right, are houses under construction and within 10 metres to the rear, is the former Abatoir. The large house, in its own grounds, opposite the white roofed building at the east end of the High Street, is the Parish Church Manse.
Courtesy of RCAHMS / RAF Air Photographs Collection

MARKET SQUARE, COLDSTREAM (ORIGINAL HEADQUARTERS COLDSTREAM GUARDS)

MARKET SQUARE 1936

The building on the right was the original headquarters of the Coldstream Guards, the second oldest regiment of foot guards in Scotland.
© *University of St Andrews Library / Licensed via www.scran.ac.uk*

COLDSTREAM 1950

Coldstream on the north bank of the River Tweed has been an important crossing point from the time it had the first ford of any consequence above Berwick. Coldstream's High Street, can be seen heading through the town towards the Tweed Bridge, the crossing into England. The Leet Water joins the Tweed on the right of the picture. Bottom right can be seen the four stage tower of the Lees Stables c.1770. Just beyond where the High Street turns right towards the bridge is the Marjoribanks Monument (1832), a doric column topped by a statue of Charles Marjoribanks MP, of the Lees. As the river meanders east towards Berwick-upon-Tweed the Lennel Estate occupies the wooded area beyond the bridge on the left.
Courtesy of RCAHMS / RAF Air Photographs Collection

SMEATON'S BRIDGE C.1890

The River Tweed and England on the south bank.
Courtesy of RCAHMS

COLDSTREAM BRIDGE C.1890

This landmark structure, east of Coldstream, provides a memorable image to those crossing the Border for the first time. Built by James Smeaton for the Tweed Bridges Trust 1763–67, the five main arches are identical in radius and link Scotland with England, at a point where the River Tweed is the national boundary. The fifth arch is partially hidden by the Coldstream Marriage House, on the Scotland side of the river, a popular venue from 1754 when declaratory marriages in England were made illegal. However, after 1856 the 'instant' wedding in Scotland was no longer permissible due to the introduction of a three-week residence qualification. The Marriage House was also where the tolls were collected until their abandonment in 1826. In 1787 Robert Burns crossed the bridge to make his first visit to England. On his return, he knelt on the bridge and gave a prayer for his native land which can be found in *The Cottar's Saturday Night*.
Reproduced courtesy of Mrs Hay / RCAHMS

COLDSTREAM 1996

The centre of the town, with the High Street right to left across the top half of the photograph.
© *Scottish Borders Council*

COLDSTREAM BRIDGE 2006

(*Right*) In 1961–62 the pilastered parapet was corbelled out, to achieve the widening of the road surface – more suitable for the increased volume of traffic on the A698.

THE SHORE,
COCKBURNSPATH C.1905
Cove Harbour houses at the base
of the access road, along with
possible local residents.
© East Lothian Museums Service
/ Licensed via www.scran.ac.uk

COTTAGES IN COVE HARBOUR 1990

Ruined cottages surrounded by the rocks of a
natural harbour, overlook a local fisherman at
work, with the distant image of East Lothian's
Torness Nuclear Power Station, on the horizon.
Crown copyright: RCAHMS

COVE HARBOUR 1995

On Berwickshire's coast at its most northerly
point, one of the most atmospheric tidal inlets on
Scotland's East Coast. The existing harbour was
completed in 1831 by Sir John Hall of nearby
Dunglass. The most interesting feature of this
'hidden treasure' is a 55m access tunnel that is cut
through the cliff from the access road and which
contains a number of cellars cut into the rock.
The exit path from the tunnel can be seen on the
opposite side from the harbour entrance. Beneath
the cliff overlooking the sand within the harbour,
are two houses that can only be accessed by foot.
Ruined cottages can also be seen within the
harbour. Cove village, top left, can be viewed at
the top of the access track.
Crown copyright: RCAHMS

Close to the Oxnam Water, 7km north east of Jedburgh. © *Scottish Borders Council*

CRANSHAWS CASTLE 1983

Cranshaws Castle, built by the Swinton family in the late 14th century. *Crown copyright: RCAHMS*

CRANSHAWS 1998

A small community on the Whiteadder Water, 15km north east of Duns. The Church dates from 1899 and is situated on a site that had at least two previous buildings. © *Scottish Borders Council*

CUMLEDGE MILL 2006

Close to Preston, north of Duns and on the side of the Whiteadder Water. The former workers houses, are a reminder of a large-scale woollen industry in the Merse. Quality blankets were produced until changing fashions in bedding witnessed the introduction of continental duvets and the ultimate demise of the Berwickshire mill in the 1960s. The mill has been demolished but Cumledge Mill House is nearby, having been built in 1854.

DERE STREET, ROMAN ROAD / ST CUTHBERT'S WAY

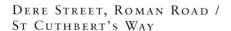

This view looks south from a point east of Lillardsedge off the A68 road, 4km south of St Boswells. The route of Dere Street can be seen following the line from bottom right of photograph towards the strip of trees that head south, bearing slightly left towards the Border and the Cheviot Hills on the horizon. Dere Street, the mediaeval name for the Roman Road, was built in the late first century AD to link the legionary fortress of York and Inchtuthil, near Perth.

The section of the Roman road, in the lower three quarters of the photograph, is now part of St Cuthbert's Way, a walking route from Melrose to Holy Island, a distance of 100km. This cross Border footpath was opened in 1996 and takes its name from St Cuthbert who was born near Melrose, of humble parentage, in 635. After being Prior at Melrose he eventually became Prior and later Bishop at Lindisfarne on Holy Island. He died on the Farne Islands in 687. *Courtesy of John Dent*

RIVER TWEED AT DRYBURGH 1998

(*Right*) The ruined abbey along with the Dryburgh Abbey Hotel shelters within the autumn tints as the River Tweed flows slowly past St Boswells, heading east. © *Scottish Borders Council*

DRYBURGH ABBEY 1997

(*Below*) On the north side of the River Tweed 15km west of Kelso. Dryburgh Abbey was founded in 1150 by Hugh de Morville, Constable of Scotland. Staffed by Monks from Alnwick and linked to nearby Melrose Abbey, by Monk's Ford. English attacks caused damage in 1322 and 1385 and the Reformation brought its active life to an end. Sir Walter Scott (1771–1832) and Field Marshall Earl Haig (1861–1928) are buried here. *Crown copyright / RCAHMS*

DUN LAW WIND FARM 2003

Looking east from Dun Law, 394m above
sea level, the twenty six 40m-high towers
and turbines dramatically dominate the
Border skyline south of Soutra Hill, 20km
south east of Edinburgh. The A68 road
traverses the site, between the two groups of
towers. Under the ownership of Scottish
Power, each unit produces 660kw using the
three-bladed turbine.
© *Scottish Borders Council*

DUNSE, JOHN WOOD 1824

*Reproduced by permission
of the Trustees of the
National Library of Scotland*

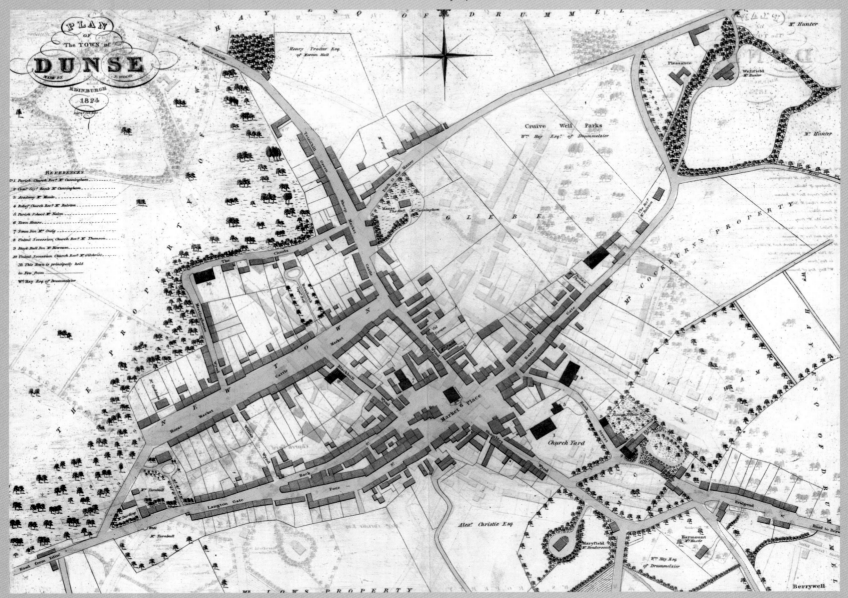

DUNS

Duns is situated in the Merse of Berwickshire, 24km west of Berwick-upon-Tweed.
Chambers noted that, 'the town originally stretched from the northern border of a lake near
Dunse Castle, called the Hen Pow, along the southern skirt of the Law, and covered no part
of its present site'.

Dunse was chartered as a burgh of barony in 1489 and was razed to the ground by
the troops of King Henry VIII in 1545. The new town was rebuilt some 500m south, where
the present day community has developed. By the early 1800s there were 2300 inhabitants,
a good market, a bleachfield and a tan-works. The railway arrived in 1849. Duns had the
distinction of being the county town of Berwickshire jointly with Greenlaw from
1853–1903 and then on its own, until the reorganization of local government in 1975.

DUNS 1948

Newtown Street, centre left of photograph, has the former Corn Exchange. Opposite is the Library, now demolished, with the Police Station and Council Offices to the right. The Parish Church is within the Kirkyard and the South Church is opposite. Blinkbonnie Lane skirts the allotments. The Market Square features the Town Hall with four clock faces. This central building is sadly missed, built 1816 and demolished in June 1966 due to problems with the erosion of the sandstone structure. *Reproduced courtesy of RCAHMS / RAF Air Photographs Collection*

1. Newton Street
2. Corn Exchange
3. Library
4. Police Station
5. Council Offices
6. Parish Church
7. South Church
8. Blinkbonnie Lane
9. Town Hall

MARKET SQUARE 1935
© *University of St Andrews Library /*
Licensed via www.scran.ac.uk

DUNS, TOWN CENTRE 1994
© *Scottish Borders Council*

DUNS 1948

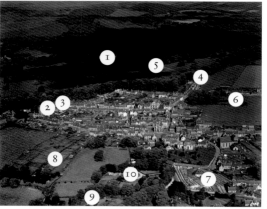

1. Duns Castle
2. Berwickshire High School
3. Vet Surgery
4. North Lodge
5. Pavilion Lodge
6. Duns Parish Church Manse
7. Livestock Market
8. Allotments
9. Market Cross
10. Maryfield

A shaft of light highlights Duns Castle amongst the trees north west of the town. At the west end of Newtown Street is the former Berwickshire High School, opened in 1896 and closed when pupils transferred to a new building on a greenfield site at the west end of the town in 1958. Behind and on the opposite side of Newtown Street at No 44 is the Vet's Surgery, now the Jim Clark Room, home to many of Clark's trophies, won during an outstanding motor racing career, including two World Motor Racing Championships, 1963 and 1965. The North Lodge c.1820 can be seen on Castle Street with Pavilion Lodge, late 1700s, nearer to the castle. Duns Parish Church Manse sits overlooking the glebe. To the south of the town is Duns Livestock Market, demolished in 1960s and Maryfield. The popular allotments are to the left. The market cross within the trees, in Duns Public Park has moved around the community. Removed from the Market Square in 1816 to make way for the construction of the Town Hall, the sandstone cross was eventually erected in the park in 1897 as part of the celebrations for Queen Victoria's Diamond Jubilee. After a full restoration, it returned to the Market Square in July 1994 when a plaque was unveiled by HM Queen Elizabeth II.
Reproduced courtesy of RCAHMS / RAF Air Photographs Collection

BERWICKSHIRE HIGH SCHOOL,
DUNS C.1930

(*Top*) *Courtesy of Robert Millican Collection*

BERWICKSHIRE HIGH SCHOOL,
DUNS 1996

(*Middle*) Opened on this west end site in 1958.
A replacement school is planned for the future.
© *Scottish Borders Council*

DUNS CASTLE 1994

(*Below*) This Gothic castle has as its core an
L-plan peel tower, built around 1320. The Castle
was bought for William Hay of Drumelzier by
his father, the Earl of Tweeddale, in 1696. This
photograph shows the building that was completed
by the architect James Gillespie Graham between
1818 and 1822. © *Scottish Borders Council*

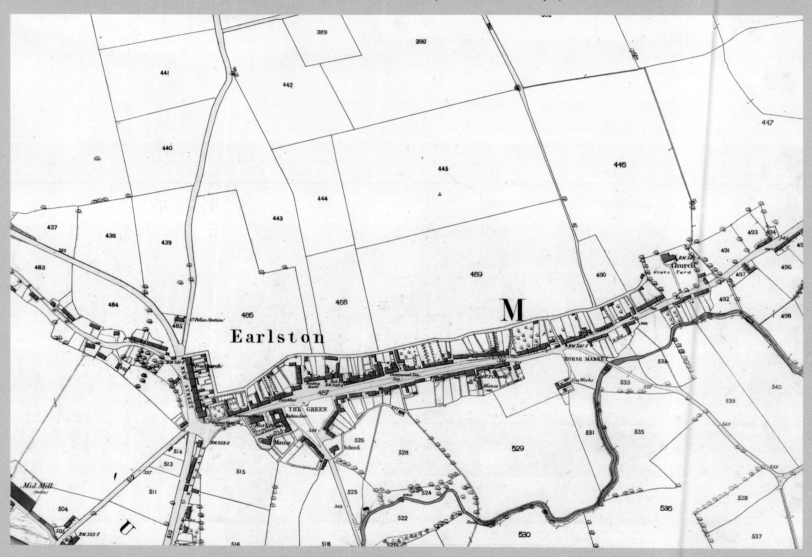

EARLSTON

Situated on the east bank of the Leader Water, 5km
north of Newtown St Boswells and on the main A68
road. This community was first recorded in the
foundation charter of Melrose Abbey, granted by King
David I in 1136 and known then as *Ercheldun* later
altered to *Ercildoun*, as confirmed when associated with
Thomas Rimour de Ercildoun, commonly known as
Thomas the Rhymer. When Roy mapped the area
around 1754, Earls Town was a settlement similar in
layout as today. By 1827 Earlston had a school and two
annual fairs of cattle. The railway arrived in 1863 via a
branch line from Ravenswood near St Boswells. A
textile mill manufactured woollens until the late 1960s.

EARLSTON 1996

The A68, is seen skirting
the west end of the village,
left of picture. High Street
crosses the photograph
from right to left to join
the A68. Kidgate is the
row of houses on the left,
immediately before the
High Street–A68 junction.
Station Road heads south
towards the wooded
area, bottom right.
© *Scottish Borders Council*

RHYMER'S MILL C.1903

Situated on the west side of the A68 and looking south in the direction of Leaderfoot, this tweed mill, on the right, was owned by Simpson and Fairbairn from 1902 until it closed in the late 1960s. The chimney, 55-60m high, was regularly painted red to protect the brick work and then demolished when coal burning boilers were replaced by diesel boilers. The wool arrived direct from the farmer to undergo the transformation to cloth, leaving the mill as a bale of tweed. Few mills in the area carried out the complete process, hence there were frequent visitors to view all aspects of tweed production under one roof. *Courtesy of Alex Blair Collection*

HIRING FAIR, EARLSTON 1934

The Hirings was a day when farm workers were contracted (hired) by a farmer to work on his farm for a period of time. The Hirings in Earlston was the first Monday in February. Hirings also took place at Duns and Kelso later in the year. As a general rule, for every 100 acres on a farm there was a farm worker and a cottage. The small tent displays a sign advertising Madame Hammond, American Palmist and Crystal Gazer.
© Scottish Borders Council / Licensed via www.scran.ac.uk

EARLSTON RAILWAY STATION C.1930
(*Above*) Opened in 1863 and situated just off Station Road on the south side of the High Street. Closed in the late 1960s. *Courtesy of Alex Blair Collection*

KIDGATE, EARLSTON, C.1910
(*Left*) Courtesy of A R Edwards

ECCLES 2003

Some 8km west of Coldstream with the Kelso, Swinton road passing through the village, from right to left. The name Eccles is derived from the Latin word *ecclesia*, meaning Church. In the eighteenth century the area was renowned for its excellent crops of wheat, barley and oats. Today the rich agricultural hinterland still produces high quality yields. The large buildings in the foreground are the base of a road haulage firm. © *Scottish Borders Council*

ECCLES C.1905

Looking towards Kelso, at the T-junction in the centre of the village. *Courtesy of Scottish Borders Archive & Local History Centre*

ECKFORD 1997

A small community halfway between Kelso and Jedburgh. © *Scottish Borders Council*

EDIN'S HALL BROCH 1997

Situated south of Abbey St Bathans in Berwickshire. This view
shows Edin's Hall Broch to the right of the complex. All that
remains is the 1.5m wall, the base that was built around the end
of the 1st millennium BC. The 5-6m thick walls still contain the
remains of a stairway and rooms. The original hillfort is hidden
by the traces of a later settlement in which embanked courts,
associated with round houses, are dominated by what was an
immense structure of a circular broch tower. The presence of
copper mines nearby is thought to have had a major impact in
transforming what was a minor hillfort into a prestigious
settlement. *© Colin J M Martin / Licensed via www.scran.ac.uk*

EDIN'S HALL BROCH 1997

*Crown Copyright reproduced courtesy of Historic Scotland /
Licensed via www.scran.ac.uk*

EDNAM 2003

A small village 3km north of Kelso close to the Eden Water, right of photograph. The Church, within the burial ground, in the foreground, has a foundation charter which dates from the beginning of the twelfth century. The school, top of photograph, looks on to the Kelso to Eccles road. James Thomson, the noted poet and a son of the manse was born in the parish in 1700. His best known poem is *The Seasons*, but he is more widely known for writing the words to *Rule Britannia*. Henry Francis Lyte was also born in the parish in 1793. He is renowned for composing the words of *Praise My Soul the King of Heaven* and *Abide with Me*. © Scottish Borders Council

EDNAM
CHURCH
2006

EYEMOUTH

A Berwickshire fishing community 4.5km north east of Ayton at the mouth of the Eye Water. The town became established as the port of Coldingham Priory from the 12th century. Due to Berwick-upon-Tweed falling into the hands of the English in 1482, the Border was drawn north of the Tweedside town, impacting on Eyemouth's development as a port. The fortifications of the 1540s, the granting of a charter to the market town in 1597–98 and its establishment as a parish by 1618 are all elements that have been crucial to the building of the character of this fishing community. John Smeaton, one of Scotland's engineering giants, was responsible for the building of a breakwater in 1768–70. Between 1770 and 1841 further improvements were made to the harbour. 1885–87 witnessed more construction with sluices at the inner end permitting the basin to be scoured.

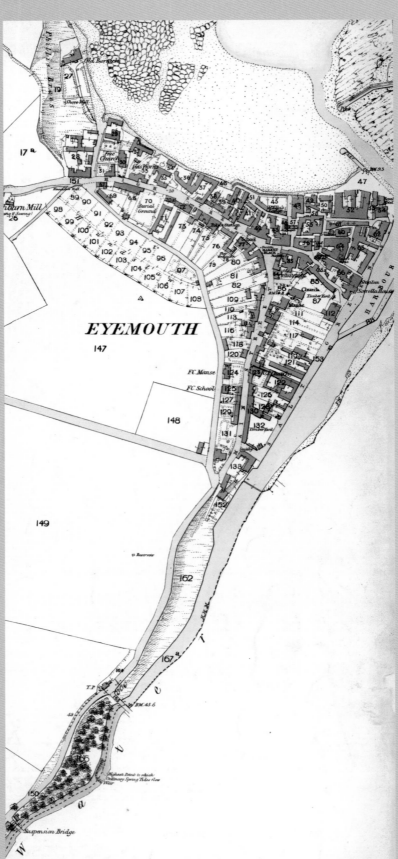

EYEMOUTH 1988

(*Opposite*) The harbour entrance then and today leads to the quayside and the mouth of the Eye Water. At the end of the main harbour can be seen the boat building and repair yards. The long white building on the north side of the harbour is the fish market. In 2006 a modern purpose built fish market occupies the site immediately left of the harbour entrance. The large building on the left of the harbour basin is Gunsgreen House (c.1755). Top right of photograph is the edge of the local industrial estate. The town's popularity as a holiday destination is confirmed by the large static caravan park, bottom right. *Courtesy of RCAHMS*

EYEMOUTH 1997

(*Above*) The golf course in the foreground with the harbour the central feature. It was from this harbour on 14th October 1881, known locally as Black Friday, that most of the local fishing fleet set sail. Tragically most were caught unaware by a great storm that claimed the lives of 189 fishermen from the Berwickshire coast, 129 coming from Eyemouth. Many boats attempted to head for the safety of the harbour but sadly most capsized or were smashed on the Hurker Rocks only metres from the harbour entrance. The Craig brothers, due to a family tragedy, did not put to sea with the rest of the fleet back in 1881. Alex Craig, a relation, recalled his life as an Eyemouth skipper for BBC Radio Tweed in 1989. © *Scottish Borders Council*

FAST CASTLE

(*Right*) A nineteenth century engraving by Patrick Nasmyth for Sir Walter Scott.
© *Scottish Life Archive / Licensed via www.scran.ac.uk*

FAST CASTLE 1997

(*Above*) Being exposed to the elements of the Berwickshire coast has progressed the deterioration of this former stronghold. The remaining stonework clings to the end of the most prominent rugged outcrop, north of St Abbs Head. This castle was first recorded in the 14th century. Both Margaret Tudor in 1502 and Margaret Stewart in 1566 stayed here when travelling to Edinburgh. It is the 'Wolf's Crag' in Sir Walter Scott's novel *The Bride of Lammermoor*. © *Scottish Borders Council*

FERNIEHIRST CASTLE

(*Right*) Situated 1.5 km south of Jedburgh. Built in 1476 by Sir Thomas Ker. Central to actions in numerous wars including being captured from the English by the French garrison of Jedburgh in 1549 only to be seized again by the English in 1570. The spiral staircases in the castle, it is claimed, turn to give the left-handed Kers an advantage to defend the upper floors from attackers After being almost completely destroyed it was rebuilt in a T-plan at the end of the 16th century. Having been occupied for close on two hundred years, it then fell into decay before being leased to the Scottish Youth Hostel Association between 1934 and 1984. After major restoration by the 12th Marquis of Lothian, the castle opened to the public in 1986. *Crown copyright: RCAHMS / Ian Lindsay Collection*

FLOORS CASTLE 2000

(*Opposite*) Overlooking the town of Kelso and the River Tweed, this is not a real castle, indeed no castle has ever stood here. Where the central block is now, an existing tower-house was transformed into a plain, but symmetrical Georgian mansion when William Adam was awarded a commission in 1721. Between 1837 and 1847 William Playfair built the pavilions on both sides creating the forecourt at the entrance. By 1849 he had transformed the central Adam mansion to conform with the rest of his design. From all angles the pepper-pot turrets, the ornate water-spouts and embattled parapets make a striking impact of grandeur of 19th century architecture. Today Floors Castle is the home of the 10th Duke of Roxburghe.
Courtesy of Roxburghe Estates

FOGO 2003

(*Top left*) 5km south west of Duns, with the Blackadder Water to the right of this small community. Fogo Kirk within the burial ground, bottom right, is the site of a church from the mid 12th century.
© *Scottish Borders Council*

FOGO KIRK WITH LYNCH GATE 2006

(*Left*) In the late 1600s the two 'lairds lofts' were probably built on, with their unusual outside stairs. The small belfry was also added around this time. Another feature of this community is the Lynch Gate, the entrance gate to the Kirk which incorporates the war memorial.

FOULDEN DEANS 1998

(*Above*) The road from Berwickupon-Tweed heads west to the Woodlands area, left of photograph. Greenlaw Farm is in the foreground with Blinkbonny to the rear and Foulden Deans on the right.
© *Scottish Borders Council*

FOULDEN 2006

(*Left*) Here in the upper village, west of the Church, the houses were nearly all rebuilt between 1850–52 and thought to reflect Flemish lines. This work was ordered by John Wilkie of Foulden House, the Laird who had an interest in architecture and had undertaken a recent continental tour. The large building on the left was the Primary School, built in 1865 and closed in 1965. The houses were once home to the schoolmaster, foreman roadman, post office, tailor, grocer, estate worker, registrar and a shoemaker. This row of houses encapsulates so many elements of Berwickshire's social history.

TITHE BARN 2006

FOULDEN 1994

A community that lies midway between Berwick-upon-Tweed and Chirnside. This recently developed area of the village, Woodlands, has Foulden Church (1786) and graveyard at the top of the photograph. In the graveyard and adjacent to the road is the Tithe or Teind Barn. The barn stored the tithes (produce) collected each year for the minister's stipend. © *Scottish Borders Council*

GAVINTON 1996

Situated two miles south west of Duns and close to the Langton Burn that flows through the wooded area in the foreground. The Greenlaw to Duns road can be seen entering right of photograph. In the second half of the 18th century the population surrounding nearby Langton House, began to increase considerably. This fact did not fit in with Lord of the Manor David Gavin's plan to remodel his policies. His solution was to build, from 1760, a fine new village, Gavinton, out of view from his own house but still convenient for the tenants and the efficient operation of the estate. The most recent Langton House, a spectacular mansion designed by David Bryce, was built in 1862 and demolished around 1950. © *Scottish Borders Council*

LANGTON HOUSE 1862

Reproduced courtesy of RCAHMS

MAIN STREET, GAVINTON 2006

Looking west.

 GORDON 1996

Situated on the Greenlaw to Earlston road 13km north of Kelso and originally called Easter Gordoun. The crossroads can be seen in the bottom right quarter of the photograph. They link Edinburgh with Kelso, top to foreground and Earlston with Greenlaw, left to right. This area became known as Wester Gordon. Later in the 19th century it became known as West Gordon and by the 20th century it was simply Gordon. The railway came to this community in 1863 linking Duns with Earlston. The station was on a site just off the top of the photograph, a short walk up Station Road from the Main Street that follows the Earlston to Greenlaw road. Gordon Primary School can be seen on the left of the picture between Main Street and the clump of trees. © *Scottish Borders Council*

MAIN STREET, GORDON C.1920

Reproduced courtesy of RCAHMS / R S Henderson collection

GREENKNOWE TOWER

To the west of Gordon and now in ruins this L-plan Tower House was built for the Setons of Touch in 1581 and still bears the initials of its builders James Seton of Touch and Janet Edmonstone. *Crown Copyright reproduced courtesy of Historic Scotland / Licensed via www.scran.ac.uk*

GRANTSHOUSE 1997

A community located 25km north-west of Berwick-upon-Tweed. The main A1 road and the east coast railway line head north from bottom left of photograph. The old post road which crossed nearby Coldingham Moor was replaced by a new section of road from Dunglass to Ayton in 1816. This route can be seen winding its way close to the village houses, bottom left, and then following the curve close to the trees where the current road sweeps south. The road to Duns can be seen crossing the railway and heading east. One of the contractors on the new 1816 road was Thomas Grant from Morayshire. Debate was generated as to where the road from Duns would join the 'new' road and it was Thomas Grant who decided on the intersection, on the road through the village, to the left of the present bypass. He built a house at this point and tradition tells us that he had a profitable additional activity selling alcohol to his navvies from the original 'Grant's House'. A map of 1826 records 'Bank Ho', Bankhouse being the original official name. For a time both Grantshouse and Bankhouse were used until the former was adopted. The North British Railway arrived in June 1846. The former Primary School, most recently an Outdoor Education Centre with football pitch, can be seen centre left of the village. © *Scottish Borders Council*

GRANTSHOUSE 2006

Looking east through the village, from the A1.

GREENLAW 1996

This village lies 12km south west of Duns in a loop of the Blackadder Water, left quarter of photograph, and at an intersection of roads in Berwickshire. The original Greenlaw was on a site 1.5km south of the present community where it became a burgh of barony in 1596 with a mercat cross from 1633. However, around 1696 the mercat cross was moved to a site in the present Greenlaw, enabling this community to become the county town of Berwickshire around 1698, replacing Berwick which had been in English hands since the late 15th century. In 1760 a turnpike road was built from Coldstream to Soutra Hill making the route through the village a staging point from Wooler to Edinburgh. In 1829 a small neo-classical County Building was built and can be seen to the right of the T-junction. After having the status of county town it reverted back to Duns in 1903. To the rear of the County Building stands the red sandstone Kirk built in 1675. The road to Duns heads north east from the top of the photograph. The Coldstream–Edinburgh road can be followed from the right to bottom left of the photograph. The Primary School stands in front of the white house on the right hand side of the Duns road.

© *Scottish Borders Council*

GREENLAW COUNTY BUILDING 1959

(*Top left*) *Crown copyright / RCAHMS*

DUNS ROAD C.1930

(*Top right*) *Reproduced courtesy of RCAHMS / R S Henderson*

HEITON

3km south of Kelso, this village retains much of the character it had a century ago.

Roxburgh Mill farm can be seen top left, overlooking the meandering River Teviot as it flows left to right, behind the trees, towards Kelso. Heiton Mains farm is at the village entrance, right of photograph. Back in the 1750s the community was known as Hightoun, predominately the homes of farm labourers. Some of the frequently changing residents, found work on the three local estates; Springwood, Ladyrigg and Sunlaws. Today the village is close to the Roxburghe Championship Golf Course at Sunlaws and a new residential development that overlooks the River Teviot.
© *Scottish Borders Council*

THE ROXBURGHE GOLF COURSE 1997

Close to Heiton Village is the Roxburghe Championship Golf Course along with the Roxburghe Hotel and Golf Club House. The River Teviot can be seen on left of photograph flowing towards the impressive Roxburgh railway viaduct. © *Scottish Borders Council*

ROXBURGHE HOTEL AND GOLF CLUB HOUSE 2002

Courtesy of Roxburghe Estates

THE HIRSEL ESTATE 1979

The Hirsel Estate, on the western outskirts of Coldstream, has been the seat of the Earls of Home since 1611. Since 1589 a house has been recorded on the present site of the Hirsel House, top right of the photograph. Recent archaeological investigations within the estate have discovered evidence of settlements dating back to Neolithic times. Most of this view is now part of The Hirsel Country Park, open to the public. The site of the walled garden, midway between the lake and Hirsel House, is a reminder of the early years of the 20th century when 12 men were employed to provide for the 'big house' and operate a commercial outlet. The Homesteads, at the corner of the lake, is now a craft centre and museum. The Hirsel Lake was excavated in the 1780s and provides an ornithologist's hide to witness hundreds of swans, duck, geese, gulls and numerous other species. At the west end of the lake is the edge of Dundock Wood, now with perhaps the best display of rhododendrons and azaleas in south east Scotland; an established annual attraction. This well known asset was

the result of a severe storm on the night of 14th October 1881, the same storm that devastated the fishing community of Eyemouth. The high winds destroyed an area of woodland next to the Greenlaw Road. Consequently a family member suggested the establishment of a plantation of rhododendrons. The acid loving plants necessitated the importing of peat from Bonkyl Estate, then owned by the Home family.

The golf course of Coldstream Golf Club is in the lower section of the photograph, with the Leet Water flowing at the east side of Hirsel House as it meanders south to Coldstream and the River Tweed. The building top centre at the top of the track is the Old Laundry with the Old Dairy directly behind. The buildings between the Laundry and Hirsel House are the Stables.

The Hirsel was the home of Rt Hon. The Lord Home of the Hirsel KT, PC, Prime Minister of the United Kingdom October 1963 to October 1964. Lord Home died in 1995 aged 92.

© Scottish Borders Council

HIRSEL HOUSE 1980

Crown Copyright: RCAHMS

45

HUME 1988

Hume Castle dominates this village, situated 8km north of Kelso. The commanding stronghold dates from the 13th century and from 1560 was the seat of the ancient and powerful Hume family. Pont's map of around 1600 records *Hooome Castle*. After being captured on a number of occasions it was finally destroyed by Cromwell's artillery under Colonel Fenwick, in 1651. The Earls of Home retired to The Hirsel in 1611. The castle's present form, a folly, was raised from the ruins by the Earl of Marchmont in 1794.
Crown copyright / RCAHMS

 ## HUNT MEET AT HUME 1963

The Duke of Buccleuch's Hunt meeting at Hume Castle. This photograph shows Huntsman Tom Smith, right, along with his whippers-in, moving the hounds off. © *Robert D Clapperton Photographic Trust / Licensed via www.scran.ac.uk*

HUTTON 1997

This small community sits 9.5km west of Berwick-upon-Tweed. The former village school is the first building on the right as you travel through the village from left to right. © *Scottish Borders Council*

HUTTON PARISH CHURCH 2006

Built in 1835, modernised in 1934 and in 1961.

HUTTON CASTLE C.1900

(*Right*) 3km south east of Chirnside on the south bank of the Whiteadder Water. Hutton Castle or Hall originated in the 16th century and was acquired from Lord Tweedmouth in 1916 by Sir William Burrell who proceeded to refurbish it to display his art. Burrell lived here from 1927 until his death in 1958. During his lifetime he amassed a huge collection of art and antiques, over 8000 items, gifting them to the City of Glasgow. After Burrell's death and as a result of his will, the principal interiors were removed and reconstructed as part of the magnificent Burrell Collection, now located in Pollok Estate, Glasgow. Despite being close to demolition, the Berwickshire Castle has survived to be once again a private dwelling. *Courtesy of Scottish Borders Archive & Local History Centre*

JEDBURGH

Situated on the Jed Water 19km north east of Hawick and 18 km south west of Kelso. When Ecred, bishop of Lindisfarne, established settlements on the banks of the Jed Water in 854, Gedwearde was the identified name. The present town developed along with the Augustinian priory that was elevated to the status of an abbey. The community became a royal burgh in the 12th century. It was at the end of the 15th century that a Jedburgh Grammar School was first recorded, an education project of the abbey, with the monks teaching boys grammar, Latin grammar! The present day secondary school is Jedburgh Grammar. Jedburgh was the county town of Roxburghshire before it was replaced by Newtown St Boswells in 1899.

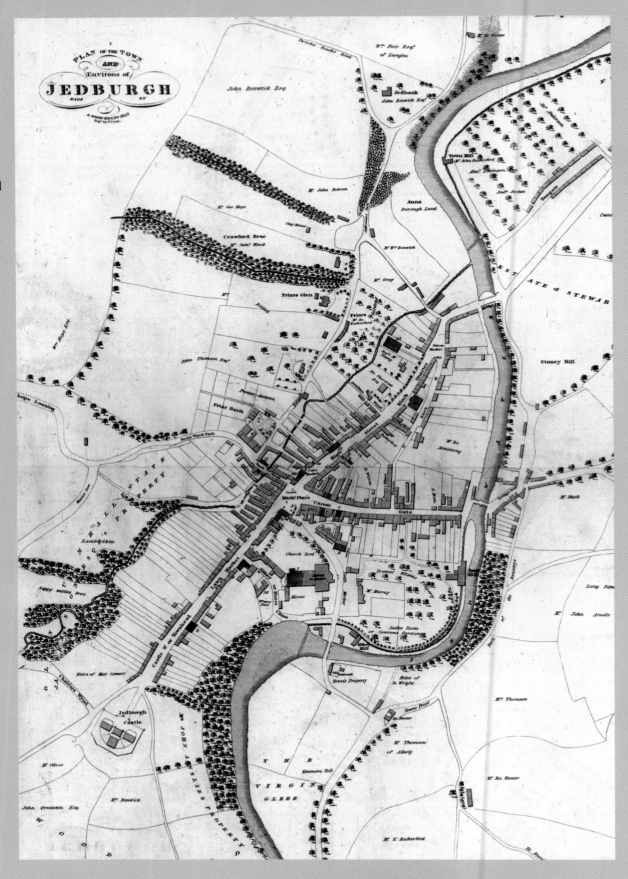

JEDBURGH, JOHN WOOD 1823

Reproduced by permission of the Trustees of the National Library of Scotland

JEDBURGH, 1949

Looking west with the
North British Rayon
factory dominating the
townscape. Built in 1929
and demolished in 1968
this manufacturer once
employed over 600
workers.
*Courtesy of RCAHMS /
Air Photographs Collection*

MARY, QUEEN OF SCOTS' HOUSE

Only a few hundred metres from the 12th
century abbey, this house was visited by Mary
in October 1566. The contents and displays
within the rooms reflect the story of Mary
Queen of Scots, 1542–87, her childhood in
France, her return to Scotland as Queen, her
stormy reign and finally her captivity at
Fotheringay Castle that ended with her
execution. © *Scottish Borders Tourist Board /
Licensed via www.scran.ac.uk*

JEDBURGH JAIL AND MUSEUM 1997

Overlooking the town at the top of the Castle Gate, this building reflects John Howard's Reformatory Imprisonment principles and dates from 1823. The three separate cellblocks could be supervised from a central point in the main building. This site was previously occupied by the Royal Castle of Jedburgh which at times was a royal residence but after numerous attacks, was demolished in 1409. The Museum displays artefacts that relate to life in a 19th century prison.
© Scottish Borders Council

JEDBURGH ABBEY 1997

10km from the Border with England, this magnificent building was founded by David I. Augustinian canons started the construction of the abbey church soon after 1138 with most of the building dating from 1180 through to the early 13th century. As Anglo-Scottish relations deteriorated, the abbey was viewed as a target, resulting in a number of devastating attacks until 1545. However, it was fortunate that the abbey avoided further damage after the Reformation in 1560 and continued to be used by the local community, until 1875. The regular use undoubtedly provided the area with the best-preserved of the four remaining Border abbeys. The Jed Water is overlooked by the abbey on what are terraced slopes. The old part of the town, with its modernised buildings, is to the rear of the abbey church.
© Scottish Borders Council

50

JEDBURGH 1993

The centre of the town lies behind the
abbey. The A68 road heads north,
skirting the right side of photograph.
Crown copyright: RCAHMS

JEDBURGH 1962

This winter scene looks north with the abbey
centre foreground and the North British Rayon
factory to the right. The Jed Water can be seen
winding its way from north to south. Castle
Gate continuing into the High Street can be seen
from bottom left across the photograph. Abbey
Close comes round behind the abbey before
bridging the Jed Water. ©*The Scotsman
Publications Ltd / Licensed via www.scran.ac.uk*

KELSO

At the confluence of the Rivers
Tweed and Teviot, this community
developed from the foundation of
the abbey in 1128. Today the
population is over six thousand
(2004) and the town combines
commerce, light industry, agriculture
and a centre for finance within
Scottish Borders. A town with an
exceptional sporting tradition where
opportunities and facilities provide a
quality experience for resident,
businessman and the visitor.

KELSO, JOHN WOOD 1823

*Reproduced by kind permission of the
Trustees of the National Library of Scotland*

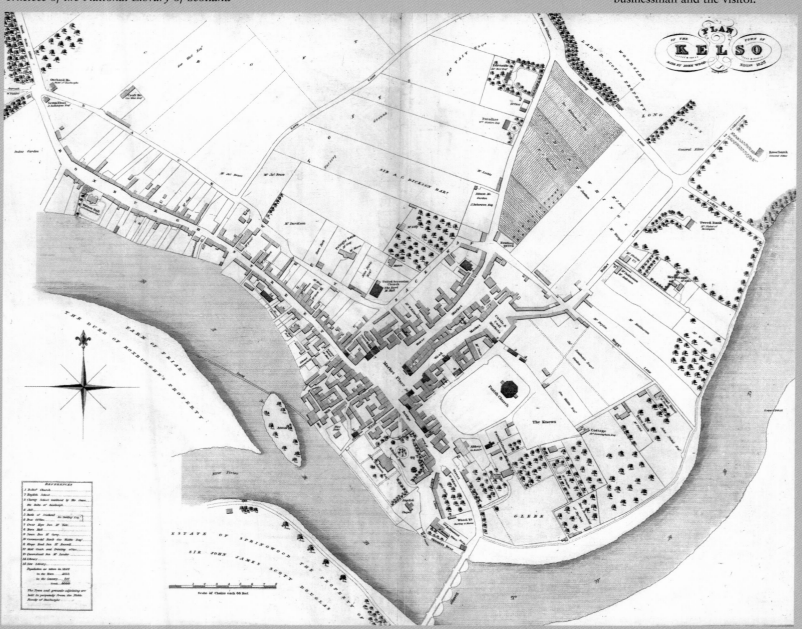

Kelso 1948

Pinnaclehill House sits on the left as it overlooks the River Tweed. Kelso High School can be seen to the rear of the town, right of the spire of St John's Church. John Rennie built the bridge between 1800 and 1803. The Junction Pool, a magnet for anglers through the centuries, is at the junction of the River Teviot and the River Tweed. In the background is Floors Castle, built in 1718 by the first Duke of Roxburghe. At the base can be seen the bridge and track of the railway linking Kelso with Berwick-upon-Tweed. The line closed after the final goods train, on March 30th 1968.
Courtesy of RCAHMS / RAF Air Photographs Collection

1. Kelso High School
2. St John's Church
3. John Rennie Bridge
4. Floors Castle
5. Railway
6. Junction Pool
7. River Teviot
8. River Tweed
9. Pinnaclehill House

1. Springwood House
2. Teviot Bridge
3. Inch Road
4. Kelso High School
5. Poyder Park
6. Friarshaugh
7. Site of Wester Kelso
8. Roxburgh Castle
9. The Square

KELSO 1948

Springwood House, demolished in 1950, is in the background, beyond the bridge over the River Teviot. Inch Road, to the right of St John's Church spire, has houses under construction with prefabs in the foreground. Kelso High School is the large building right of photograph, overlooking Poynder Park. Friarshaugh is the site of the Royal Burgh of Roxburgh from 1124, where existed a Royal Mint, Corn Mills, a Church and a Grammar School, supervised by the Abbot at Kelso Abbey. By the 1500s residents had moved across the river to Wester Kelso and eventually the old burgh disappeared. A recent archaeological dig confirmed elements of the former community. No obvious trace of the the Royal Burgh exists today. *Courtesy of RCAHMS / RAF Air Photographs Collection*

KELSO ABBEY 1996

The ruins of Kelso Abbey, founded
by David I, dominate this entrance
to the town. In the foregound is the
L-shaped Memorial Cloister, burial
ground of the Dukes of Roxburghe.
Close by is the Sir Robert Lorimer
designed War Memorial with the circular
base. Originally the largest of all the
Border abbeys, with both eastern and
western transepts but sadly now the
smallest, for only the western transept,
tower and two bays of the south arcade
of the nave, remain. It was to this site in
1128, a community of Tironian
(Benedictine) tradesmen monks moved
from Selkirk and built the magnificent
Kelso Abbey. 10th August 1460
witnessed the coronation of the eight
year old King James III at the high altar.
1523 saw the abbey suffer at the hands
of Lord Dacre's men. 1545 saw the Earl
of Hertford's men further destroy the
abbey 'so that the enemy may have little
use for it'. After five days most of the
building was destroyed and many lives
had been lost. 1649–1771 it was used as
a parish church with a thatched roof
covering part of the transept. The ruins
are now in the care of Historic Scotland.
© *Scottish Borders Council*

DRAWING OF KELSO ABBEY

By A F Morse in 1923, from details
supplied to the Vatican in 1517, prior to
near complete distruction in 1545.

KELSO 1990

(*Opposite*) The River Tweed with John Rennie's Bridge,
brings traffic from the south past the ruin of Kelso
Abbey into Kelso Square. The abbey originally extended
to the right, as far as the present day car park. St
Andrew's Episcopal Church, 1870, can be seen between
the abbey and the River Tweed. Kelso Parish Church,
circular roof, is within the trees to the right of the
abbey. Ednam House Hotel, with helicopter parked in
grounds, faces the river. Top left is Poynder Park,
home to Kelso Rugby Club. The long white buiding,
top right, is Edenside Primary School.
Crown copyright / RCAHMS

KELSO 1997

The south bank of the River Tweed with
housing developments that commenced in
the 1970s. John Rennie's bridge crosses the
River Tweed. © *Scottish Borders Council*

KELSO 1998

Looking east, the River Tweed
sweeps through the town and
heads for Coldstream passing
under the new Hunter Bridge,
opened in August 1998.
© *Scottish Borders Council*

KIRK YETHOLM 1998

13km south-east of Kelso and 3km from the English border, this village has a village green at its centre and it is situated on the opposite bank of the Bowmont Water from its twin-village, Town Yetholm. The house to the left of the continuous row of houses in the left corner is known as the 'Gypsy Palace'. The village was home to the Faa family, the royal house of the gypsies who died out in the 19th century. Sir Walter Scott modelled his famous character Meg Merrilies on Jean Gordon, wife of Patrick Faa. The Pennine Way, 432km long distance footpath from Eadale in the Peak District National Park, enters the village passing the 'Gypsy Palace' to terminate on the green. The local Church sits within the Churchyard, top left of photograph. The village is also on St Cuthbert's Way, the long distance footpath that follows an Anglo-Scottish east–west route from Melrose to Lindisfarne on Holy Island. © *Scottish Borders Council*

MAIN STREET, KIRK YETHOLM C.1915

Looking east towards the village green. *Courtesy of Scottish Borders Archive & Local History Centre*

LADYKIRK 2003

9km north east of Coldstream and north of the cross-border Swinton to Norham road on the north bank of the River Tweed. This village has as its central feature the Kirk of Our Lady of the Steill, or as it is now called , Ladykirk Church.
© *Scottish Borders Council*

LADYKIRK PARISH CHURCH, A MEDIEVAL CHURCH

This church originated, so legend goes, when King James IV of Scotland was nearly drowned crossing the ford, just below the Church. He, it is claimed, vowed to build a Church in memory of the Blessed Virgin of the Steill who had saved him. A steill is a deep pool where salmon nets are placed. By March 1500 the building had commenced with stone from nearby Swinton Quarry. The king did visit to view progress and attended a service in 1505. The twenty large buttresses were essential to support the weight of the roof with its overlapping stones of wrought ashlar. The upper section of the tower was designed by William Adam and completed in 1743. Further embellishment was the addition of the clock, a gift from Lady Marjoribanks, in 1882. © *John R Hume / Licensed via www.scran.ac.uk*

LAUDER

The small town of Lauder can be found 13km south of Soutra Hill, straddling the A68 road. Lauder gained a charter as a Royal Burgh in 1298 and then re-chartered in 1328 and again in 1502. This typical Scottish Burgh developed in a pattern that has hardly changed to this day. The Tolbooth, later known as the Town Hall, overlooks the Market Place. By the late 1790s Lauder was a post town with over 1000 inhabitants and a branch of the Bank of Scotland opened in 1833. In 1896 the local council laid out a nine hole municipal golf course. From 1901 to 1932 there was a light railway link to Fountainhall, on the main Galashiels to Edinburgh line. By the early 20th century the population had dropped to just over 700. At the beginning of the 21st century the housing base is once again expanding.

LAUDER 1952

1. Lauder Parish Church
2. Lauder School
3. Middlemiss cart shed
4. Roadmen's houses
5. Allotments
6. Cottesbrooke
7. War-disabled houses

Keeping a watchful eye over the community is Thirlestane Castle, the home of the Maitland family since around 1590. Between 1664 and 1667 Sir William Bruce, the architect, remodelled the house for the 2nd Earl, later the Duke of Lauderdale. The house was again modernised in 1840 with the addition of the main wings on the west front. In the late 1970s, having been inherited by Captain The Hon. Gerald Maitland-Carew, further major work was carried out. The castle and its collection are now in a Trust.

In the centre of the photograph is Lauder's Parish Church, a most unusual form, a Greek cross with four equal arms spreading from a central crossing with a tower. This Kirk has the north gable dated 1673, built by Sir William Bruce for the Duke of Lauderdale who had simply requested that it be a 'decent and large enough, with a handsome little steeple'. The local school sits at the west end of the kirkyard. To the left of the school is the Middlemiss cart shed and next door are the two roadmen's houses with the allotments owned by Colonel Fleming. The large house in the foreground is Cottesbrooke along with its large garden. The houses opposite Cottesbrooke were occupied by families of the war-disabled. *Courtesy of RCAHMS / RAF Air Photographs Collection*

Lauder 1952

West High Street is between the shops and houses across the centre of the photograph. Stow Road disappears towards the moor, passing the parkland area of Allanbank on the left. The Edinburgh road heads right and out of picture. The Row is the short road joining the intersection from bottom right. Formerly 'Rue de Roi', this was the original entrance to Thirlestane Castle. More allotments can be seen to the rear of the houses at the intersection.
Courtesy of RCAHMS / RAF Air Photographs Collection

1. West High Street
2. Edinburgh Road
3. The Row

1. Mid Row
2. Wyndhead Farm
3. Factor's house
4. Cottesbrooke

LAUDER 1952

Looking from the south, the main A68 Jedburgh to Edinburgh road heads north passed the central area of the town, divided by a line of buildings known as Mid Row. At the north end of Mid Row, overlooking the Market Place, can be seen the tower of the 18th century Town Hall where the part-vaulted ground floor was the burgh prison until 1843. The set of buildings, bottom left, is Wyndhead Farm. The Factor's house is at the road junction with Cottesbrooke viewed to the left. The broadleaved trees on the right are within the policies of Thirlestane Castle.
Courtesy of RCAHMS / RAF Air Photographs Collection

LAUDER, HIGH STREET, c.1900

(Top) © Robert D Clapperton Photographic
Trust / Licensed via www.scran.ac.uk

LAUDER, MARKET PLACE 1935

(Above) © University of St Andrews Library /
Licensed via www.scran.ac.uk

LAUDER 1996

The A68 road heads south, from top of
photograph, with the Stow Road joining from
the right. © Scottish Borders Council

LEADERFOOT 1996

The River Tweed heads east under the third and
most recent bridge that carries the A68 road
north, at the established crossing point known
as Leaderfoot. The seventeenth-century three-
arched sandstone Newstead Bridge, in the
shadow of the most recent structure, is open
only to pedestrians and cyclists but still
impresses with its strength and design. The
largest of the three structures, the Victorian
railway viaduct, serves as a magnificent reminder
of a former railway era when the North British
Railway's 'Waverley Line' linked Edinburgh and
Carlisle. © *Scottish Borders Council*

⌂ LEITHOLM 1998

In the Merse of Berwickshire, 8km north-west of Coldstream and on the main A699 road from Kelso to Berwick-upon-Tweed, left to right across the photograph. The elongated Main Street reflects a character of housing that developed from a group of huts in the mid-eighteenth century. Kames West Mains farm can be seen at the side of the Charterhall road as it heads towards the top of photograph. Mersington Farm is in the top left corner. The stream at the west end of the village is the Lambden Burn that flows into the Leet Water. The field on the south side between the bridge and the village was known as flooders, as it frequently flooded. The annual shows were held here up to the 1930s and it also served as the local quoiting field. © *Scottish Borders Council*

LEITHOLM 2006

The west end of the village.

10km north west of Duns on the
Dye Water that flows in front of
the row of houses in centre of the
photograph. Longformacus
House, early 18th century, stands
in its own grounds overlooking
the village. Partially hidden in the
trees in front of the house is the
Parish Church, rebuilt in 1730 in
a basic rectangular form with fine
stained glass, especially the
Landale memorial window.
© *Scottish Borders Council*

MANDERSTON HOUSE 1993

(*Opposite*) 2.5km east of Duns and the home of Lord and Lady Palmer. The grounds are laid out around an artificial lake, top of picture. The original Georgian House, built in the 1790s, was acquired by Sir James Miller in the late 1890s and he commissioned John Kinross to rebuild the house (1903–05). Today it's one of the finest Edwardian country houses in Scotland complete with stuccoed ceilings, marble floors and a silver-railed staircase. Below stairs the Edwardian sophistication is evident in the kitchens, the housekeeper's room and the manservant's room. The terraced gardens, also designed by John Kinross, are still planted in the Edwardian style. Out of picture, on the left, are remarkable courtyard stables designed by John Kinross (1895), with marble floors and teak stalls, perhaps the best example of equine accommodation anywhere.
Crown copyright: RCAHMS

MARCHMONT HOUSE 1976

(*Above*) 5km south west of Duns this Palladian house was built for the 3rd Earl, probably by John and Robert Adam, to designs by their father William (1750–54). Alterations were undertaken in 1834 and Sir Robert Lorimer (1913–20) added a top storey. This property is now a residential care home.
Crown copyright: RCAHMS

MAXTON 1997

South of the River Tweed, left, and 13km west of Kelso. Back in 1545 Maxton was destroyed by the Earl of Hertford, after the English lost at the Battle of Ancrum Moor. By 1587 it had recovered and was made a Burgh of Barony by Ker of Littledean, the major landowner. Main Street is the through road from Kelso to St Boswells, top to base of photograph. The Maxton Cross, parts of which are probably 13th century, and the former smiddy, overlook the site of what was a triangular village green. The recently refurbished village hall, originally the library and reading room, was built in 1909, through the generosity of the philanthropist Andrew Carnegie.
© *Scottish Borders Council*

MAXTON CROSS 2006

The cross, that had major restoration work in 1881 by Sir William Ramsay Fairfax, Bart. Little remains of the village green.

ꔦ MELLERSTAIN HOUSE 1983

11km north west of Kelso. The house was started by George Baillie of Jerviswood and his wife Grizel by engaging William Adam to design the two square wings in 1725. The present house, the main block, was linked to the Adam wings between 1770–78 and designed by Robert Adam. The resulting castellated mansion is thought to be one of the great Georgian houses in Scotland.

The Italian-style terraced gardens, laid out by Sir Reginald Bloomfield in 1909, can be seen at the front of the house, above the lawn that stretches down to the artificial lake. The 13th Earl of Haddington, John Baillie-Hamilton, transferred the ownership of Mellerstain, his home, to a charitable trust in 1986, to ensure its future. *Crown copyright / RCAHMS*

73

MERTOUN HOUSE 1996

3km east of St Boswells and thought to have been designed by Sir William Bruce in 1703. In 1843 William Burn was responsible for the construction of a south wing, note the c.1910 photograph. This was not balanced until 1913–16 when Gibson and Gordon added another building to the north, resulting in the two additions somewhat overwhelming the Bruce original. A major scheme saw Ian Lindsay (1953–56) commissioned to demolish the wings and return the mansion to its original proportions, the house as it is today. Set within twenty acres of beautiful grounds, the house

overlooks the north bank of the River Tweed, left of photograph. The meadow, extending from the front of the house, is separated from the driveway, by a Ha Ha. This is a wall, built from the stone from the former wings, below road level and around the edge of the meadow along with a broad ditch. This feature, completed in 1958, prevents any livestock accessing the roadway. The impression given from the house is that the meadow is level with the road surface. Today, Mertoun House is home to the 7th Duke of Sutherland.
© Scottish Borders Council

Mertoun House, Nr. St. Boswells.

MERTOUN HOUSE c.1910
© Robert D Clapperton Photographic Trust

MONTEVIOT HOUSE 2006

Viewed from the south bank of the River Teviot.

MONTEVIOT, LOOKING EAST 2001

4km north of Jedburgh the River Teviot meanders east passing Monteviot House, the seat of the Marquis of Lothian. Built as a farmhouse in the 17th century with subsequent Marquises of Lothian leaving their mark, each adding to the building. An arboretum as well as rose, water and herbaceous gardens attract visitors during the summer months. Lothian Estates whose grounds surround the house, feature colour coded walks, emanating from the nearby Harestanes Visitor Centre.
© *Scottish Borders Council*

MOREBATTLE 1998

A small village nestling in a loop of the Kale Water, top right, and in the shadow of the Cheviot Hills, some 11km south of Kelso. The name means the dwelling on the lake, 'mere' being a lake or loch, 'botl' or 'bodl' from the Anglian, meaning a house or dwelling. Prior to the nineteenth century there existed a substantial loch between Morebattle and Linton, before being drained. The Parish Church (1757) with graveyard is on the upper right. Main Street runs from the centre to upper left, passing the school, opened in 1931. The road off the Main Street, before the school and heading in the direction of the Kale Water, top right, is Teapot Street. The road heading to top right is Toongate. The road opposite is Mainsfield Avenue while the road entering the village from bottom right is called the Pikin Stanes. St Cuthbert's Way, the long distance walking route, passes through here on its way from Melrose to Lindisfarne. Today the village's population is around 266.

© Scottish Borders Council

MOREBATTLE C.1900

Courtesy of Scottish Borders Archive & Local History Centre

MOREBATTLE LOOKING EAST.

NENTHORN 2003

6km north of Kelso on the Kelso to Carfraemill road that exits bottom right. The last building, heading north, on the left, is the former school.
© *Scottish Borders Council*

NEWTON DON 1996

3km north of Kelso, built 1817–20 and designed by Sir Robert Smirke. The stables and market garden are to the rear. The Eden Water flows behind the stables.
© *Scottish Borders Council*

NEWTOWN ST BOSWELLS 1996

The former A68 road twists its way from south to north through this central Borders community. The auction mart can be seen spread out across the top right of the photograph. The construction of the railway and resulting station along with the mart, in the early 1850s, triggered the expansion of the village. The railway closed in 1969 and this coincided with the building of new offices for County Council employees, the modern flat roofed building with tower, upper centre. Today this building is the headquarters of Scottish Borders Council, a major employer. The road that exits left, south of SBC offices, heads for Bowden, with the transport yard of Scottish Borders Council on the left. In 1993 the A68 eastern bypass was constructed, bottom right, thus reducing the volume of traffic in the village.
© *Scottish Borders Council*

NISBET 1997

This small scattered village is situated 6km north east of Jedburgh. The River Teviot at top of picture can be seen close to the former track of the Jedburgh to Roxburgh railway when it crosses the road some 40m from the bridge.
© *Scottish Borders Council*

OXNAM 1997

Small village 6km south east of Jedburgh. This image shows the road across the picture from right to left travelling from north to south. Oxnam Water, within the tree area, exits right and heads north to join the River Teviot close to Crailing. © *Scottish Borders Council*

RURAL PAXTON

Eastern Berwickshire looking north in September
1997, the harvest has been gathered in and Paxton
House overlooks the River Tweed. Paxton village
can be seen in the background. The land on the
opposite bank from Paxton House is England, as
the Border follows the River Tweed at this point.
© *Scottish Borders Council*

PAXTON HOUSE 1997

6km west of Berwick-upon-Tweed with a magnificent south-facing setting overlooking the River Tweed. Dates from 1758 and built by Patrick Home of Billie for his intended bride Sophie de Brandt. Designed by John and James Adam under the supervision of James Nisbet. This is a fine Scottish Palladian mansion. The central red sandstone house with four-column portico is flanked by two courtyards, kitchen on the left and stables to the right. The house contains a fine collection of furniture by Thomas Chippendale and William Trotter. Since 1993 the picture gallery has been an outstation of the National Galleries of Scotland. The grounds were laid out from 1767 by Robert Robinson, a one-time assistant to 'Capability Brown'. Paxton House is now managed by the Paxton Trust. © *Scottish Borders Council*

PAXTON HOUSE C.1870

The main entrance. *Courtesy of RCAHMS / Paxton House Trust*

PAXTON 2003

This estate village of picturesque cottages has some older properties pantiled. The village continues to expand. In the past, bricks, tiles and drain pipes were made on the estate. © *Scottish Borders Council*

SCHOOLERS ROW 2006

PEASE BAY 1994

South of Cove Harbour, close to the boundary with East Lothian and at the point where the Pease Burn enters the North Sea. A holiday centre with static homes.
© *Scottish Borders Council*

PENIEL HEUGH

Standing on the site of an iron age fort, 5km north of Jedburgh, the extinct volcanic intrusion of Peniel Heugh has the Waterloo Monument at 237m above sea level, a Border landmark. The 48m tower was raised by the Marquis of Lothian to commemorate the Battle of Waterloo (1815). William Burns' design commenced construction in 1815 but collapsed in 1816. Today's monument was designed by Archibald Elliot and completed, 1817–24.
© *Scottish Borders Council*

POLWARTH C.1900

6km south west of Duns and just over 6km north of Greenlaw. Formerly an extensive settlement with 14 cobblers. The central element disappeared in the early 20th century. All that remains are some houses outwith the former settlement, along with Marchmont House and Polwarth Kirk.
© *University of St Andrews Library*

POLWARTH KIRK 2006

It was Sir Patrick Hume, first Earl of Marchmont, who rebuilt the present Church with the addition of a Tower in 1703. The family vault beneath the Kirk, to be seen through grating at the east gable, was where Sir Patrick was concealed for over a month in 1684. This action was taken due to his association with his friend Robert Baillie of Jerviswood who had been arrested for treason linked to a plot to assassinate Charles II. Lady Grisel Baillie, Hume's daughter, carried food to her father and, 'enlivened his solitude with all the home news and amusing stories'.

PRESTON 1994

A small village 4km north of Duns.
The Gifford to Preston road enters
from bottom left of photograph
while the Duns road exits bottom
right. Preston Farm is within the
village with Bonkyl Lodge in the
trees at the top of the photograph.
© *Scottish Borders Council*

REDPATH 1996

On the east side of the Leader Water, 3km south of Earlston. The one and only street has farm buildings at both ends. Noticeably there is only one entry and exit point, at the base of the photograph. © *Scottish Borders Council*

REDPATH C.1927

Courtesy of A R Edwards

RESTON C.1990

On the Eye Water 4km from Coldingham. By the 1600s it had four water mills. A single linear settlement that had by the 1830s an Inn used for the change over of horses on the Great North Road from Scotland to England. The North British Railway opened the mainline station in 1846 which finally closed in 1966. On the right of the photograph can be seen the Mart. However, the first mart started at Howies Yard next to Swan House opposite the railway station. Established in 1875 by Messrs R G Swan and J B Kellie who set up in partnership at Reston and nearby Duns. In 1946 the firm amalgamated with the Berwick Auction Mart Company. By 1992 the level of sales had dropped but the closure of the Fatstock Auction Mart at Berwick-upon-Tweed saw Reston benefiting with guaranteed sales on Tuesdays and Fridays. The Mart finally closed on 16th February 2001. *Courtesy of Reston Primary School*

RESTON C.1950

Main Street. *Courtesy of Robert Millican Collection*

RIVER TEVIOT

This river of the Scottish Borders rises in the foothills of White Hope Edge on the border with Dumfries and Galloway, some 6km west of Mosspaul. It flows north east through Teviotdale past Teviothead, then to Hawick and Roxburgh before joining the River Tweed at Kelso. The River Teviot provides fishing for brown trout. This image captures the river as it flows towards the Teviot Bridge, right of photograph, and then to its confluence with the River Tweed four hundred metres down river. © *National Museums of Scotland / Licensed via www.scran.ac.uk*

RIVER TWEED 2002

The River Tweed is a central feature of the Scottish Borders as it is here at Scott's View, looking towards the Eildon Hills. The Tweed has had a major impact on the development of the physical landscape and the distribution of settlements. Fourth longest river in Scotland as it flows the 156km from its source at Tweeds Well, to England and its mouth at Berwick-upon-Tweed. A slow current along with deep pools interspersed with shallow banks of gravel and pebbles has kept the Tweed free from river traffic. As a consequence of being a shallow river, few bridges span its course and many fords have served as crossing points. The shallow pools and gravel banks have made this one of Scotland's most celebrated salmon rivers.
Reproduced by courtesy of
VisitScotland Borders

⌒ ROXBURGH 1997

Situated on the River Teviot, some 6.5km up river from Kelso. This was the first Roxburgh community and called 'Auld' Roxburgh, 900 years ago. The *town* of Roxburgh was at the confluence of Teviot and Tweed at Kelso and was declared a Royal Burgh in the 12th century by King David I.

Crossing the River Teviot is the Roxburgh viaduct built in 1847 for the North British Railway Company (NBR) and its line from Kelso to St Boswells. The railway line closed in 1968. In the centre of the field between the track and the village is the ruin of Wallace's Tower, a 16th century stone

L-plan tower house. The Church and burial ground can be seen within the village. The former school, closed in 1985, is on the southern edge of the burialground. The 15th green of the Roxburghe Championship Golf Course can be seen to the right of the viaduct.
© *Scottish Borders Council*

ROXBURGH CASTLE 1974

(*Opposite*) The remaining fragments of walls of this former Border stronghold are located between the River Teviot, foreground, and the River Tweed in the background, close to Kelso. The existence of the castle has been recorded from 1125. After the capture of David I's grandson, William the Lion, by the English in 1174, an English garrison occupied the fortress until 1189 when the burgh of Roxburgh passed back into the control of the Scots king. For over a hundred years it was then a focal point of Scottish politics. In 1282 the royal marriage of Lord Alexander, the son of Alexander III, and Margaret de Dampiere, daughter of the Count of Flanders, took place within the historic walls. However, Lord Alexander died young in 1284 impacting on the succession to the crown of Scotland. By the end of the 1200s the English were again in control of Roxburgh Castle.

The Black Douglas, Sir James Douglas, recaptured the castle in 1313. The battle of Halidon Hill in 1333 resulted in Roxburgh once again returning to English occupation. The close proximity to England and its strategic importance reflected the inevitability of repeated capture. Alexander Ramsay in 1342 regained Roxburgh for the Scots king only to see the English returning in 1356. It was in 1460 that James II attacked the castle, using large cannons. Tragically, a cannon exploded resulting in a piece of the weapon fatally injuring the king. The siege continued as Queen Mary travelled from Edinburgh with the young James III. Kelso Abbey saw the crowning of James III after the castle was secured and destroyed. Sadly, by 1544 little remained of one of Scotland's greatest medieval castles.
Crown copyright: RCAHMS / John Dewar collection

ROXBURGH CASTLE
PLAN 16TH CENTURY

Reproduced courtesy of the Duke of Rutland / RCAHMS

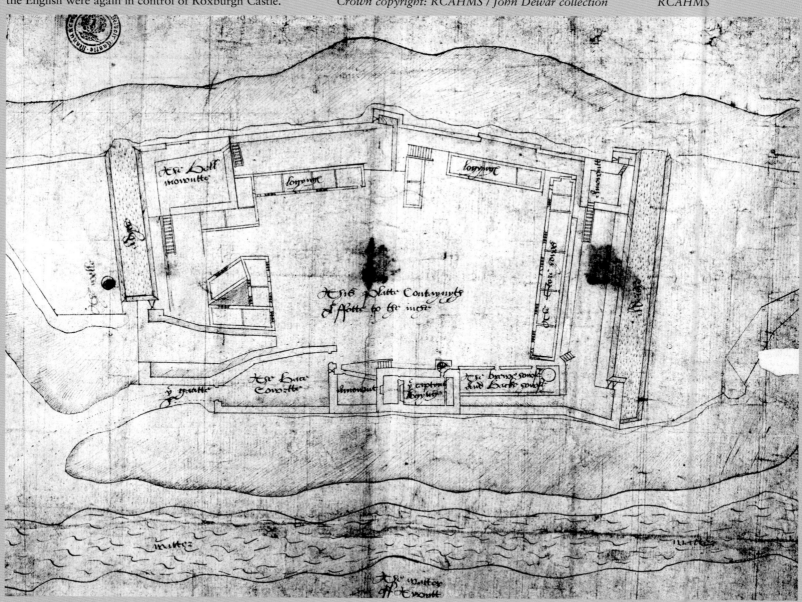

SMAILHOLM MAINS
1996

Smailholm Mains farm
in the foreground with
Smailholm village in the
centre and in the distance,
on the right amongst the
trees, Mellerstain House.
© *Scottish Borders Council*

SMAILHOLM 1996

This small village lies 9.5km north west of Kelso and has been an agricultural community throughout the centuries. From Old English 'smael' and 'ham', meaning narrow village. The village school, second building on the left as you enter from bottom right, closed in 1970. A mill on the nearby River Eden is recorded in the 1200s, a building used extensively during the following 600 years. The road from bottom left to top right links Earlston to Kelso while the road exiting at the base, leads to Gattonside. Top left is Smailholm House an early 18th century laird's house. © *Scottish Borders Council*

SMAILHOLM TOWER 1999

10km north west of Kelso, close to Sandyknowe
Farm. This early 16th century, five-storey, 17m
high tower commands a prominent location in
the Borders landscape. The surrounding basalt
crags, provided the building stone. This
stronghold of the Pringle family was sold by the
descendents of Andrew Pringle in 1645 when
Smailholm estate was acquired by the Scotts of
Harden. However, they abandoned the tower in
favour of the nearby Sandyknowe, a familiar
abode to Sir Walter Scott in his early years. This
fine example of a Border Peel Tower is in the care
of Historic Scotland. *Courtesy of RCAHMS*

SMAILHOLM TOWER 1996

*© The Rourke Collection /
Licensed via www.scran.ac.uk*

SOUTHERN UPLAND WAY, LAUDER 1990

The marker pole guides walkers towards Lauder on this section of the 341km coast to coast footpath, linking Portpatrick in Galloway to Cockburnspath in Berwickshire. *Courtesy of Keith Robeson*

SPROUSTON 2003

Formerly a centre for weaving, 3km east of Kelso. The white building in the centre is the Primary School. The village green can be seen between the school and the white Sprouston Church in the foreground.
© *Scottish Borders Council*

SPROUSTON STATION C.1970

Opened in 1851 by the York, Newcastle & Berwick Railway, as part of their line from Tweedmouth. One of only two railway stations built in Scotland by an English railway company. © *RCAHMS / Licensed via www.scran.ac.uk*

🎧46 St Abbs Fishery
c.1910

(*Above*) Looking north
from Pettico Wick.
Courtesy of RCAHMS

Sea View Terrace,
St Abbs c.1900s

(*Right*) © *Peter Nisbett /
Licensed via www.scran.ac.uk*

ST ABBS / COLDINGHAM SANDS 1989

Berwickshire coastline with St Abbs in the foreground and Coldingham Sands in the bay, back right. 5km north of Eyemouth, the sea and shoreline at this point attract divers to the St Abbs and Eyemouth Voluntary Marine Reserve.
Crown copyright: RCAHMS

ST ABBS 1989

(*Above*) This harbour was constructed between 1833–35 at Coldingham Shore, which was renamed St Abbs. The harbour is a haven for pleasure craft and a base for lobster and crab fishing. The local Church, built in 1892, can be seen top right. The RNLI inshore lifeboat station building is within the outer harbour. *Crown copyright: RCAHMS*

ST ABBS HEAD 1997

(*Below*) St Abbs Head National Nature Reserve is owned by The National Trust for Scotland. This dramatic Berwickshire headland, north of St Abbs village and harbour, hosts the St Abbs Lighthouse that was built by David and Thomas Stevenson (Thomas's son was R L Stevenson, Scots author and poet) and illuminated from 1862. This crucial light was automated in 1993. The area also has the largest colony of cliff-nesting seabirds in south-east Scotland. The cliffs provide a spectacular viewing point to observe guillemots, kittiwakes, razorbills, shags, fulmars and herring gulls. The valley occupied by the Mire Loch, to be seen in front of the yellow gorse, separates the sedimentary rocks, common to most of the Borders, from the hard volcanic rocks of St Abbs Head. The most northerly coastal outcrop of rock supports the sparse ruins of Fast Castle. © *Scottish Borders Council*

Situated in the Central Borders on the south bank of the River Tweed and opposite Dryburgh Abbey. The original village has completely disappeared from its site 1km south east of the present community. In the early 1600s *Lessiddinn* (Lessudden House) was recorded on Pont's map and it was not until the mid 1700s that present day St Boswells began to develop into a village. Benrig Cemetery was attached to the demolished church of Lessudden. The name St Boswells was derived from the medieval church dedicated to St Boisil, who was a prior of Melrose Abbey. The photograph shows the main A68 road as it skirts the west end of the village, along with the central avenue of trees, planted by the Duke of Buccleuch, to commemorate the Diamond Jubilee of Queen Victoria. What is reputedly the largest village green in Scotland can be partially seen beyond the avenue, on the right of the photograph.
© *Scottish Borders Council*

(*Opposite*) Jenny Moore's Road, from base of photograph, follows a line to the centre of the village. Behind the village can be seen the River Tweed and Dryburgh Abbey, within the trees.
© *The Scotsman Publications Ltd / Licensed via www.scran.ac.uk*

STICHILL 1996

5km north of Kelso and about 125m above sea level this village commands a superb view south over the Tweed Valley, towards the Cheviots and England. The Kelso–Greenlaw road enters from the left and passes the Parish Church on the left, then the former entrance to Stichill House, before travelling through the village, sweeping left to leave top right. The road that exits bottom right leads to the village of Ednam.
© *Scottish Borders Council*

〔51〕 SWINTON 1997

(*Above*) In the Merse of Berwickshire 8km south-east of Duns. A planned village set around its rectangular village green, to the right. The green has in its centre the village Cross (1769), a classical sundialed column. Morningbank can be seen to the rear of the village.
© *Scottish Borders Council*

SWINTON WEST END C.1930S

(*Middle Right*) At the T junction in main photograph. Main Street looking east with the former United Free Church in the background, with its spire complete. *Reproduced courtesy of RCAHMS / R S Henderson*

VILLAGE GREEN C.1920

(*Right*) The cross can be seen on the right. *Reproduced courtesy of RCAHMS / R S Henderson*

🐴²⁹ 🐴⁴⁸ 🐴⁵³ 🐴⁵⁷ 🐴⁵⁸

TOWN YETHOLM 1998

11km south of Kelso, on the opposite side of the upper Bowmont Water from its twin-village, Kirk Yetholm. Yetholm means the 'place at the gate' from the old Scots 'yett' meaning gate and 'holm' or 'ham', the Anglo-Saxon for settlement. The nearby Bowmont Water generated a long line of water-powered mills involved in corn-grinding and saw-milling. The triangular village green can be seen to the right of the main street, that leads to Morebattle and heads out of the top of the photograph. The road to Kirk Yetholm skirts the caravan park and exits left. The local school is at the base of the photograph. © *Scottish Borders Council*

TOWN YETHOLM 1926

Setting off on a day trip on a charabanc. The first of the three vehicles was owned by John Turnbull from Kelso. © *Fred Kennington / Licensed via www.scran.ac.uk*

UNION BRIDGE 1981

The oldest surviving carriage suspension bridge in Britain.
Built across the River Tweed in 1819–20, 8km upstream from
Berwick-upon-Tweed, on the stretch where the Scotland–
England boundary travels along the centre of the river, north
of Horncliffe, Northumberland. 133m between the suspension
points, 5.5m wide and with what was a revolutionary
wrought-iron link for the chain cables, invented by the bridge
designer Captain Sir Samuel Brown. The design of this
structure influenced Thomas Telford in the construction of the
Menai Suspension Bridge. *Crown copyright / RCAHMS*

WESTRUTHER 1996

Close to the head of the Blackadder Water in north west Berwickshire on the southern edge of the Lammermuir Hills, this small community is 12km west of Lauder at an altitude of 215m. The village school can be seen at the bend of the road, top left quarter of photograph. © *Scottish Borders Council*

WHITSOME 1998

(*Opposite*) In the Merse district of Berwickshire 4km south of Allanton and 10km south east of Duns. The road through the village to Chirnside, exits right. © *Scottish Borders Council*

WHITSOME C.1910

(*Below*) Courtesy of Scottish Borders Archive & Local History Centre

WHITSOME.